WORKBOOK

FOR

UNOFFENDABLE

How Just One Change Can Make All of Life Better

(A Practical Guide to Brant Hansen's Book)

Mindful Forge

THIS WORKBOOK BELONGS TO

This companion Workbook is intended to be used as a supplement to the original book. It is not meant to replace the original book, but rather to enhance and deepen the understanding of the concepts presented in the original book

Table Of Contents

HOW TO USE THIS WORKBOOK **8**
QUICK SUMMARY **11**
BEING UNOFFENDABLE: THE RIDICULOUS IDEA **13**
Key Lessons 15
Self-Reflection Questions: 16
Life-Changing Exercises: 20
EVERYONE'S AN IDIOT BUT ME **22**
Key Lessons 23
Self-Reflection Questions: 24
Life-Changing Exercises: 28
SIX BILLION RINGS **30**
Key Lessons 31
Self-Reflection Questions: 32
Life-Changing Exercises: 36
ARTISTS SEE THINGS **37**
Key Lessons 38
Self-Reflection Questions: 39
Life-Changing Exercises: 43
BERT AND ERNIE AND SATAN **45**
Key Lessons 46
Self-Reflection Questions: 47
Life-Changing Exercises: 51
BEAUTIFUL EXCEPTIONS **53**
Key Lessons 53
Self-Reflection Questions: 54
Life-Changing Exercises: 58

THE WORLD'S WORST BEDTIME STORY **60**
Key Lessons 61
Self-reflection Questions: 62
Life-changing Exercises: 66
AIN'T YOU TIRED? **68**
Key Lessons 69
Self-Reflection Questions: 69
Life-Changing Exercises: 74
REVEREND OF THE DUMPSTER **76**
Key Lessons 77
Self-Reflection Questions: 78
Life-Changing Exercises: 82
IDEA: LET'S PUNCH BRANT IN THE FACE **83**
Key Lessons 84
Self-Reflection Questions: 85
Life-Changing Exercises: 89
ATHEISTS, SOCIALISTS, AND TOAST **90**
Key Lessons 92
Self-Reflection Questions: 92
Life-Changing Exercises: 97
ANGER'S FUN—EXCEPT FOR THE BOILING, BLAZING, AND BURNING PART **98**
Key Lessons 99
Self-Reflection Questions: 100
Life-Changing Exercises: 104
THE BIG QUESTION: WHAT ABOUT INJUSTICE? **106**
Key Lessons 107
Self-Reflection Questions: 108
Life-Changing Exercises: 112

THIS IS THE CHAPTER ABOUT HOW WE'RE JUST BARELY SMART ENOUGH TO BE STUPID 113
Key Lessons 114
Self-Reflection Questions: 115
Life-Changing Exercises: 120
NOTHING LEFT TO LOSE 122
Key Lessons 123
Self-Reflection Questions: 123
Life-Changing Exercises: 127
AND HERE'S THE CHAPTER I KEPT PUTTING OFF . . . 129
Key Lessons 130
Self-Reflection Questions: 130
Life-Changing Exercises: 134
WE'RE ALL WAITING FOR SOMETHING . . . THAT ALREADY HAPPENED 136
Key Lessons 137
Self-reflection questions: 138
Life-changing exercises: 142
ON WINNING—AND BY "WINNING," I MEAN, OF COURSE, LOSING 144
Key Lessons 145
Self-reflection questions: 145
Life-changing exercises: 149
THE WORLD'S WORST NEIGHBOR 151
Key Lessons 151
Self-Reflection Questions: 152
Life-Changing Exercises: 156
IMBALANCED? YOU BETTER HOPE SO 158

Key Lessons 159
Self-Reflection Questions: 159
Life-Changing Exercises: 163
I CAN WORSHIP A GOD LIKE THAT 165
Key Lessons 166
Self-Reflection Questions: 166
Life-Changing Exercises: 171
HERE'S THE PART WHERE I TALK ABOUT SOME DANISH PEOPLE 172
Key Lessons 173
Self-Reflection Questions: 174
Life-Changing Exercises: 178
FORGET DANISH PEOPLE—LET'S TALK ABOUT YOUR ELBOW 179
Key Lessons 180
Self-Reflection Questions: 181
Life-Changing Exercises: 185
AND LO, THE KINGDOM OF GOD IS LIKE A TERRIBLE FOOTBALL TEAM 187
Key Lessons 188
Self-Reflection Questions: 189
Life-Changing Exercises: 193
SELF EVALUATION 195

HOW TO USE THIS WORKBOOK

Welcome to the companion Workbook for "Unoffendable" by Brant Hansen! This workbook is designed to help you dive deeper into the key lessons and life-changing principles presented in the main book. Here's a simple guide on how to make the most out of this resource:

1. Start with the Summary: Begin each chapter by reviewing the summary of the corresponding chapter in the original book. This will refresh your memory and provide context for the lessons and exercises ahead.

2. Explore Key Lessons: Dive into the key lessons from the main book presented in each chapter of this workbook. These distilled insights will highlight the essential concepts you need to understand for personal growth and transformation.

3. Reflect with Self-Reflection Questions: Take time to engage with the self-reflection questions provided after each chapter summary. These questions are designed to prompt deep introspection and help you apply the book's principles to your own life circumstances.

4. Practice Life-changing Exercises: After reflecting on the key lessons, put them into action with the life-changing exercises included in each chapter. These practical activities are designed to empower you to implement positive changes in your attitudes, behaviors, and relationships.

5. Conclude with Self-Evaluation Questions: At the end of the workbook, you'll find self-evaluation questions. Use these prompts to assess your progress, identify areas for improvement, and celebrate your growth along the way.

6. Go at Your Own Pace: Remember, personal growth is a journey, not a race. Take your time to work through each chapter thoughtfully and thoroughly. Feel free to

revisit previous chapters as needed and adapt the exercises to suit your unique circumstances.

By actively engaging with the content of this workbook, you'll not only deepen your understanding of "Unoffendable" but also cultivate a greater sense of self-awareness, resilience, and compassion in your daily life. Enjoy the journey, and may this workbook be a valuable companion on your path to personal growth and transformation.

QUICK SUMMARY

In "Unoffendable," author Brant Hansen explores the transformative power of choosing to live without offense. Through personal anecdotes, biblical insights, and practical advice, Hansen illustrates how embracing a mindset of unoffendability can revolutionize one's life.

The book begins with Hansen's own journey of discovering the freedom that comes from relinquishing the right to be offended. Drawing from his experiences as a radio host and Christian, Hansen highlights the pervasive nature of offense in society and the detrimental effects it can have on relationships, mental health, and spiritual well-being.

Hansen challenges the reader to reconsider common misconceptions about anger and offense, arguing that they are not inherent or necessary aspects of the human experience. Instead, he proposes that choosing humility and forgiveness leads to greater peace and fulfillment.

Throughout the book, Hansen emphasizes the importance of understanding the true source of one's significance and security. He encourages readers to shift their focus away from seeking validation from others and instead find their worth in God's unconditional love.

Furthermore, Hansen addresses the practical implications of living unoffended, offering strategies for dealing with conflict, managing expectations, and cultivating genuine empathy for others. He emphasizes the role of self-awareness and intentional decision-making in maintaining a non-offensive mindset.

Ultimately, "Unoffendable" presents a compelling argument for embracing humility, forgiveness, and grace in all areas of life. By making the simple yet profound choice to let go of offense, individuals can experience greater freedom, joy, and fulfillment in their relationships and daily interactions.

BEING UNOFFENDABLE: THE RIDICULOUS IDEA

So, here's a thought that might seem a bit out there: what if you could actually choose not to be offended?

I remember hearing this idea at a business meeting once, and it stuck with me for a few reasons: firstly, it was entirely new to me; secondly, it's rare for something from a meeting to stick in my mind; and thirdly, I was surprised I even got invited to the meeting in the first place.

The notion that we can actively decide not to take offense seemed absurd to me at first.

But as I mulled it over, I found myself considering its validity, despite my initial resistance. Isn't it strange how we often feel entitled to our anger, believing it's justified? Yet, upon reflection, I realized this entitlement may not be as justified as I once thought.

Let's be clear: anger isn't always a bad thing, but the way we often cling to it, nurturing our sense of moral superiority, might not be as righteous as we believe.

So, instead of brushing off the idea of unoffendability, I delved deeper. And to my surprise, I found merit in the concept. Choosing to let go of offense isn't about denying injustices or suppressing emotions; it's about releasing the grip of resentment and embracing a mindset of forgiveness and humility.

Sure, it's not easy, and it goes against the grain of our natural inclinations. But as I began to explore this idea further, I discovered its transformative power. By relinquishing our right to anger, we open ourselves up to a deeper understanding of grace and a more profound connection with others.

So, while some may dismiss the idea of unoffendability as foolishness, I urge you to consider its potential. It's not about denying the reality of wrongdoing or injustice; it's about transcending our instinctual responses and embracing a more compassionate way of being.

Ultimately, the choice is yours: cling to anger and resentment, or embrace unoffendability and the freedom it brings. It may not be the easiest path, but it's certainly one worth exploring.

Key Lessons

1. Choosing to be unoffendable may seem absurd at first, but it challenges us to reconsider our natural inclination to take offense and hold onto anger.
2. The idea of forfeiting our right to be offended and embracing unoffendability aligns with principles of humility and forgiveness, even in the face of perceived injustices.
3. Despite societal norms and cultural acceptance of anger, there's a call to relinquish our entitlement to anger and resentment, as it impedes our spiritual and emotional growth.

4. The notion of "righteous anger" is questioned, highlighting the tendency to justify our own anger while condemning others', and the need to surrender our claims to resentment.
5. While anger may seem justified or even necessary, there's a compelling argument for its release, as it hinders our ability to love, forgive, and empathize fully.

Self-Reflection Questions:

1. How do you typically respond when someone offends or angers you?

____

____

____

____

2. Have you ever considered the possibility of choosing not to be offended? What challenges or opportunities does this idea present for you?

3. Reflect on a recent situation where you felt justified in your anger. In hindsight, how could you have responded differently to cultivate a spirit of unoffendability?

4. Consider your beliefs about "righteous anger." How do these beliefs influence your interactions with others, especially those who have wronged you?

5. What steps can you take to release any lingering resentment or anger you may be holding onto? How might embracing unoffendability enhance your relationships and overall well-being?

Life-Changing Exercises:

1. Keep a journal for one week to track instances where you felt offended or angry. Reflect on each situation, considering alternative perspectives and responses that align with unoffendability.

2. Practice the "pause and ponder" technique: when faced with a potentially anger-inducing situation, pause before reacting and ask yourself, "Is this worth my peace of mind?"

3. Engage in a forgiveness meditation or prayer session, focusing on releasing any resentment or anger towards yourself or others. Allow yourself to experience the freedom that comes with forgiveness.

4. Reach out to someone with whom you've had a conflict or disagreement. Initiate a conversation with the intention of understanding their perspective and extending grace and forgiveness.

5. Create a visual reminder of your commitment to unoffendability, such as a mantra or affirmation displayed in a prominent place. Use this reminder to reinforce your choice to let go of anger and embrace compassion.

EVERYONE'S AN IDIOT BUT ME

In this narrative, the author admits to his inclination towards self-righteousness and resentment, shaped by his conservative upbringing and religious background. Despite acknowledging the existence of right and wrong, he challenges the notion of entitlement to anger and emphasizes the need to relinquish it. Reflecting on personal experiences, he observes humanity's tendency to perceive oneself as morally superior while condemning others. He highlights the universal habit of taking offense, fueled by a desire for righteousness. However, he advocates for a radical shift towards unoffendability, rooted in humility and forgiveness.

The author shares anecdotes illustrating his own struggles with anger and judgment, emphasizing the fallibility of human perception. He references biblical teachings and psychological research to underscore the inherent biases in human reasoning. Ultimately, he advocates for a humble approach, acknowledging the limitations of personal judgment and choosing not to take offense preemptively. Embracing humility, he suggests, leads to greater peace and understanding in interpersonal interactions.

Key Lessons

1. Acknowledge personal tendencies towards self-righteousness and resentment, shaped by upbringing and religious background.
2. Embrace humility by recognizing personal culpability and refraining from entitlement to anger.
3. Challenge the natural inclination to judge others while considering oneself morally superior.
4. Advocate for letting go of offense, emphasizing the energy and peace gained from forgiveness and unoffendability.
5. Highlight the limitations of human judgment and the importance of humility in recognizing one's own fallibility.

Self-Reflection Questions:

1. Have you ever caught yourself feeling morally superior to others? How did that influence your interactions with them?

2. In what situations do you typically find yourself quick to anger or offense? What underlying beliefs or assumptions might be driving those reactions?

3. Reflect on a recent conflict or disagreement. How did your initial judgment of the situation compare to your understanding after hearing the other person's perspective?

4. How often do you consider the possibility that you might not have all the facts or understand someone else's motives fully? How might this awareness impact your interactions with others?

5. Are there areas of your life where you could practice greater humility and forgiveness? What steps could you take to cultivate a mindset of unoffendability?

____

____

____

Life-Changing Exercises:

1. Keep a journal for a week to track moments when you feel tempted to judge or become offended. Reflect on these instances to identify patterns and underlying triggers.
2. Practice active listening in conversations by intentionally seeking to understand the other person's perspective before forming judgments or responses.
3. Engage in a daily gratitude practice to cultivate a mindset of appreciation and humility, focusing on the positive aspects of your interactions and relationships.
4. Challenge yourself to refrain from gossip or negative talk about others for a week. Notice how this impacts your thoughts and feelings towards them.

5. Volunteer or engage in acts of kindness towards others without expecting anything in return. Reflect on how these experiences shape your perceptions and attitudes towards others.

SIX BILLION RINGS

Michael, an evangelical Christian, defied cultural norms by opening a coffee shop in a liberal downtown area, embracing diverse perspectives. Despite potential clashes, he welcomed an art exhibition, previously hosted in his building, that featured controversial pieces. His gesture of hospitality, including funding catering, surprised organizers accustomed to rejection. At the exhibit, Michael's warmth and acceptance fostered a positive atmosphere, challenging the expectation of Christian offense. His approach exemplified forgiveness and love, even towards those who held opposing beliefs. By relinquishing anger and offense, Michael showcased a transformative alternative to societal expectations. Drawing from C.S. Lewis's wisdom, he emphasized the soul's vulnerability to anger's corrosive effects. Through forgiveness, he proposed a path to freedom from anger's grip, envisioning a community known for its unoffendable spirit. This ethos, he believed, would liberate individuals and promote genuine connection, transcending moral judgments. Ultimately, Michael's example urged a collective release of anger, likening it to shedding the destructive power of the One Ring in "The Lord of the Rings."

Key Lessons

1. Emphasize the power and appeal of choosing not to take offense.
2. Illustrate through Michael's example the transformative impact of embracing love and forgiveness.
3. Highlight the contrast between societal expectations of anger and offense with the liberating alternative of forgiveness and humility.
4. Echo C.S. Lewis's insight on the corrosive nature of anger and the importance of forgiveness.
5. Encourage letting go of offense and embracing forgiveness as a pathway to a less stressful and more fulfilling life.

Self-Reflection Questions:

1. How do societal expectations influence your responses to situations where you feel offended or angry?

2. Reflect on instances where you've witnessed someone respond with love and forgiveness instead of anger. What was the impact of their actions?

3. Consider C.S. Lewis's warning about the consequences of holding onto anger. How does this resonate with your own experiences?

4. Explore your attitudes towards forgiveness and offense. Are there areas where you struggle to let go of anger? Why?

5. Imagine a world where forgiveness and humility were more prevalent than anger and offense. How might this change your interactions and relationships?

Life-Changing Exercises:

1. Practice forgiveness daily by consciously letting go of minor offenses and grievances.
2. Engage in acts of kindness towards those who have wronged you, seeking to understand their perspective and extend empathy.
3. Reflect on past experiences of anger and offense, identifying patterns and triggers to help cultivate a greater sense of self-awareness.
4. Explore literature or teachings on forgiveness and humility to deepen your understanding and practice of these virtues.
5. Take practical steps to address any unresolved anger or offense, such as seeking counseling or reconciliation with those involved.

ARTISTS SEE THINGS

Perceiving beyond offense enhances our perspective, allowing us to view individuals in refreshing ways. During my stint as a baseball announcer, I often subbed for John, a respected colleague known for his professionalism and devout Christianity. John's demeanor contrasted sharply with Bill, a former player prone to profanity and rough behavior. Observing their interaction, I marveled at John's tolerance. Despite Bill's coarse manner, John surprised him with a personalized plaque, embodying unconditional acceptance.

Similarly, my friend Chris possesses an artistic vision, transforming discarded cardboard into intricate creations, like a globally-themed nativity scene. His ability to envision potential transcends material limitations. Likewise, a real estate agent, faced with a dilapidated property, envisioned its transformation into a charming home, a vision realized by its owner, Al.

God's perspective surpasses ours, enabling Him to envision redemption amidst chaos. Like a loving father,

He sees our potential despite our flaws. Jesus exemplifies this by loving even the morally flawed, like Peter, who denied Him. Jesus saw beyond Peter's betrayal, promising him a place of honor in His kingdom.

God's insight challenges us to love unconditionally, trusting His vision for each individual. Even those we find challenging may harbor unseen potential, revealed through God's perspective. Embracing unoffendability opens doors to profound connections and transformative relationships, mirroring God's unconditional love for us.

Key Lessons

1. Offense clouds our perception, hindering our ability to see the true potential in people.

2. Individuals with an artistic mindset possess the gift of envisioning possibilities beyond the surface, akin to Chris creating beauty from discarded materials.

3. God's perspective transcends human limitations, allowing Him to see the inherent value and potential in every individual, despite their flaws.

4. Choosing to adopt an "unoffendable" attitude empowers us to love others deeply, following the example of Jesus, who loved even the most morally compromised individuals.

5. God sees beyond our faults and failures, envisioning the transformed and redeemed versions of ourselves, just as He did with Peter despite his denials.

Self-Reflection Questions:

1. How does my tendency to take offense impact my ability to perceive the potential in others?

2. In what areas of my life can I cultivate a more artistic mindset, seeing possibilities where others see limitations?

3. Do I believe that God sees the best in me, even when I struggle to see it myself?

4. How can I emulate Jesus' example of loving others unconditionally, despite their flaws and shortcomings?

5. What steps can I take to seek God's perspective on the people I find most challenging or offensive?

Life-Changing Exercises:

1. Practice reframing your perceptions of others by intentionally looking for their positive qualities and potential, regardless of initial impressions.

2. Engage in a creative activity, such as art or writing, that encourages you to see beyond the surface and imagine new possibilities.

3. Spend time in prayer and meditation, asking God to reveal His perspective on the people and situations that trigger offense or judgment within you.

4. Actively seek opportunities to demonstrate unconditional love and acceptance toward those who may challenge or offend you, recognizing their inherent worth in God's eyes.

5. Keep a gratitude journal where you regularly write down qualities or actions in others that you appreciate or admire, fostering a mindset of appreciation and openness towards different perspectives.

BERT AND ERNIE AND SATAN

In the Gospels, Jesus never reacts with shock or disbelief at human behavior, indicating His deep understanding of human nature. Understanding the inherent flaws of humanity can help us adopt a less offended outlook, recognizing the prevalence of selfishness and moral failings. Despite our capacity for evil, people often express surprise at others' actions, ignoring historical and biblical evidence of human nature. Jesus, as the epitome of wisdom, foresaw and accepted human imperfections without judgment. Similarly, experiencing constant criticism, whether in Christian radio or everyday interactions, reveals humanity's inclination towards judgmentalism. Embracing the reality of human brokenness, like Jesus did, enables us to let go of offense and cultivate realistic expectations. Recognizing the universal tendency towards self-righteousness, irrespective of religious affiliation, promotes a more balanced perspective on human behavior. Ultimately, relinquishing perpetual offense aligns with Jesus' understanding of human nature and fosters a more peaceful existence.

Key Lessons

1. Jesus' lack of shock at human behavior underscores His deep understanding of human nature, setting an example for followers to adopt a similar perspective.
2. Recognizing the inherent flaws of humanity, such as selfishness and untrustworthiness, can help individuals become less easily offended and adjust their expectations accordingly.
3. Despite the prevalence of moral failings and evil in the world, people often express surprise at others' actions, reflecting a persistent naivety about human nature.
4. Embracing realistic expectations about human behavior, informed by Jesus' insight into the human heart, can lead to a more balanced and peaceful existence.

5. Constant criticism and judgment from others, whether in professional or personal contexts, highlight humanity's tendency towards self-righteousness and the need to let go of offense.

Self-Reflection Questions:

1. Have you ever found yourself surprised or shocked by someone's behavior, despite knowing the inherent flaws of human nature?

2. How do your expectations about human behavior align with your understanding of Jesus' perspective on human nature?

3. In what ways do you tend to express judgment or self-righteousness towards others, consciously or unconsciously?

---

4. How does your reaction to criticism or offense reflect your ability to embrace realistic expectations about human behavior?

---

5. Are there areas in your life where adjusting your expectations and letting go of offense could lead to greater peace and understanding?

Life-Changing Exercises:

1. Keep a journal for a week, documenting instances where you find yourself surprised or offended by others' behavior. Reflect on whether these reactions align with your understanding of human nature and Jesus' perspective.
2. Engage in regular meditation or prayer focused on cultivating empathy and understanding towards others, especially those whose actions or behaviors you find challenging.

3. Practice forgiveness towards those who have offended or criticized you, recognizing their humanity and inherent flaws.
4. Seek out opportunities to engage in compassionate listening and non-judgmental dialogue with others, fostering understanding and empathy.
5. Challenge yourself to consciously adjust your expectations about human behavior in various situations, focusing on embracing realistic perspectives informed by Jesus' insight into human nature.

BEAUTIFUL EXCEPTIONS

The Christian worldview diverges from cynicism as it celebrates the remarkable goodness humans can exhibit amidst their flaws. Instances like sincere apologies, selfless acts, and forgiveness stand out as beautiful exceptions in a flawed world. Noteworthy examples include a forgiven accident, exemplifying grace, and a widow forgiving her husband's killer, reflecting profound love. Despite brokenness, gratitude replaces offense when recognizing divine intervention and anticipating restoration. The extraordinary, like a captive audience singing praise in an oppressive prison, epitomizes grace transcending boundaries. Amidst judgmentalism, embracing exceptional acts of kindness cultivates joy and diminishes offense, emphasizing the coexistence of gratitude and wonder over anger.

Key Lessons

1. The Christian worldview finds hope in the goodness displayed by humans amidst their flaws, contrasting with cynicism.
2. Acts of humility, sacrifice, forgiveness, and kindness stand out as beautiful exceptions in a broken world.
3. Recognizing these exceptions fosters gratitude, replacing shock and anger with appreciation for the positive.
4. Instances of grace breaking through boundaries, such as in a brutal prison, exemplify the transformative power of love.
5. Embracing moments of beauty and love diminishes offense, cultivating a spirit of gratitude and wonder.

Self-Reflection Questions:

1. How do you respond to acts of kindness and forgiveness in your life? Do you appreciate them or take them for granted?

---

2. In what ways can you adjust your expectations and cultivate gratitude amidst the brokenness of the world?

3. Have you experienced moments where grace transcended boundaries, and how did it impact your perspective?

4. Reflect on times when you've been quick to judge others. How can you shift towards a more compassionate and understanding mindset?

5. Consider instances where you've been offended or angered. How might choosing gratitude instead enhance your overall well-being and perspective?

Life-Changing Exercises:

1. Keep a gratitude journal for a week, noting down at least three beautiful exceptions or acts of kindness you encounter each day.

2. Practice forgiveness by intentionally letting go of any lingering resentment or anger towards someone who has wronged you.
3. Engage in a random act of kindness each day for a week, seeking opportunities to brighten someone else's day.
4. Take time to meditate or pray daily, focusing on themes of grace, love, and gratitude to foster a more positive outlook.
5. Reflect on a challenging situation or conflict from your past, and write a letter of forgiveness or reconciliation to anyone involved, even if you don't plan to send it.

THE WORLD'S WORST BEDTIME STORY

In Sheldon Vanauken's memorable tale from "A Severe Mercy," two dogs, Gypsy and Snowball, enjoy an idyllic life in the countryside with a loving master. Despite their obedience, Gypsy's temptation to chase rabbits leads her astray, eventually causing her to run off into the woods, never to return. Snowball, however, remains faithful and continues to thrive under the master's care.

This story, though unconventional for bedtime, carries a deeper message about choosing obedience and the consequences of straying from what is right. It parallels the choice humans face in serving God or pursuing alternative paths, highlighting the importance of trust and obedience in God's guidance for a fulfilling life.

Similarly, online disagreements present two options: engaging in contentious arguments or choosing to remain unoffended and at peace. Opting for the latter promotes a more restful existence, rooted in the understanding that God is ultimately in control and patient with all individuals, even those with whom we disagree.

Reflecting on personal experiences, such as a confrontation with a fellow church member, underscores the significance of not letting offense fester. Deciding not to be offended leads to a more peaceful life, aligning with Jesus' promise of rest for those who follow him.

Ultimately, the bedtime story serves as a reminder of the goodness of the master, encouraging trust and obedience in God's guidance for a fulfilling life.

Key Lessons

1. The story of two dogs, Gypsy and Snowball, illustrates the consequences of yielding to temptation and straying from obedience to their master.

2. Gypsy's repeated disobedience led to her being leashed while Snowball continued to enjoy freedom, emphasizing the importance of trust and obedience.
3. Choosing to be unoffendable and practicing patience with others leads to a more restful life, even in the face of disagreement or insult.
4. Jesus offers rest from religious burdens and teaches simple principles that lead to a more peaceful life when practiced.
5. Ultimately, individuals have the freedom to choose whether to follow God's teachings for a flourishing life or to pursue their own desires.

Self-reflection Questions:

1. Have you ever experienced the consequences of yielding to temptation, like Gypsy in the story?

2. How do you typically handle disagreements or insults online or in person, and does it bring you peace or restlessness?

3. Reflect on a time when you held onto offense or grudges for a long time. How did it affect your mental and emotional well-being?

4. Consider Jesus' teachings about simplicity and rest. In what areas of your life can you simplify and find more peace?

5. Think about your freedom to choose how to live your life. Are there areas where you feel torn between following God's principles and pursuing your own desires?

Life-changing Exercises:

1. Practice choosing to be unoffendable for a week. When faced with a potentially offensive situation, consciously choose to respond with patience and kindness.

2. Simplify your daily routine by identifying and eliminating unnecessary tasks or commitments that cause stress or busyness.

3. Spend time in reflection and meditation on Jesus' teachings, particularly the Sermon on the Mount. Consider how you can apply these principles to your daily life for greater peace and rest.

4. Engage in acts of kindness and forgiveness towards others, even those who may have wronged you in the past. Notice how releasing resentment contributes to your overall sense of well-being.

5. Have a conversation with a trusted friend or mentor about areas in your life where you struggle to trust and obey God's guidance. Seek their perspective and support in aligning your actions with your beliefs for a more fulfilling life.

AIN'T YOU TIRED?

Living a restful life in our culture can seem unusual, yet it's a path my wife and I have chosen, albeit imperfectly. Rejecting a prestigious law career for family time defied societal norms, leading to a job with less pay but more family time. Despite criticism, our choice to prioritize family over busyness stood out in our neighborhood, where others noticed our relaxed lifestyle. This lifestyle choice, characterized by "doing nothing," defies the norm of constant activity and busyness. Jesus offers rest from societal pressures, urging us to resist the cultural current of busyness and status-driven living. By surrendering control and dropping the need to constantly prove ourselves, we can find rest and let go of anger and resentment. Trusting in God's sovereignty and ceasing our efforts to control others leads to a more peaceful existence. As Aibileen's words in "The Help" resonate, constantly evaluating others and holding onto anger is exhausting. Choosing rest over the pursuit of validation and control ultimately brings greater peace and fulfillment. So, ain't you tired of the endless pursuit of validation and control?

Key Lessons

1. Living a restful life in a culture driven by busyness and achievement can be countercultural and attract attention.

2. Choosing family time and simplicity over prestigious career paths can lead to a more fulfilling life, despite societal pressure.

3. Embracing a lifestyle of "doing nothing" can foster deeper connections with neighbors and inspire reflection on spiritual matters.

4. Jesus offers rest from the relentless pursuit of status and validation, urging followers to resist cultural norms and find peace in surrendering control.

5. Trusting in God's sovereignty and letting go of anger and resentment can lead to a more restful and fulfilling life.

Self-Reflection Questions:

1. Have you ever felt pressured to prioritize achievement and busyness over spending quality time with loved ones?

2. How do you respond to societal expectations and pressures that conflict with your personal values and priorities?

3. In what ways do you seek validation and control in your life, and how does this impact your sense of peace and fulfillment?

4. Reflect on moments when you've held onto anger or resentment. How did it affect your relationships and overall well-being?

5. Consider your beliefs about rest and spirituality. Do you prioritize time for quiet reflection and connection with something greater than yourself?

Life-Changing Exercises:

1. Take a day or weekend to intentionally slow down and prioritize rest and relaxation. Notice how it feels to step away from the busyness of everyday life.

2. Practice forgiveness by writing a letter to someone you've been holding a grudge against, expressing your feelings and offering forgiveness.

3. Create a list of your values and priorities in life, then evaluate how your actions align with them. Make adjustments as needed to live more authentically.

4. Engage in a regular spiritual practice that allows you to connect with something greater than yourself, whether through prayer, meditation, or nature walks.

5. Seek out opportunities to build deeper connections with your community, whether through volunteering, joining a club or group, or simply reaching out to neighbors.

REVEREND OF THE DUMPSTER

Once, a pastor, prior to the internet boom, secretly indulged in adult magazines during his wife's absence, despite knowing it was wrong. Frustrated by his addiction, he disposed of the magazines when his wife left on a trip. Later, he regretted his actions and attempted to retrieve them before her return, but accidentally fell into the dumpster, breaking his arm. His wife discovered him trapped, highlighting his humiliation. Reflecting on this, I ponder if his marriage endured and if forgiveness prevailed. It prompts me to envision a church of individuals acknowledging their faults, akin to AA meetings or Celebrate Recovery groups, fostering camaraderie and understanding. Jesus' teachings underscore our universal fallibility, challenging notions of righteousness. He exposes our self-deception, urging reliance on God's judgment and mercy. Jesus dismantles self-righteousness, demanding humility and forgiveness. Ultimately, embracing this truth liberates us from anger and self-justification, aligning us with His radical grace.

Key Lessons

1. Acknowledging our faults and seeking forgiveness liberates us from the burden of pretense and self-righteousness.
2. Embracing the reality of our own fallibility fosters empathy and understanding towards others.
3. Jesus' teachings challenge the notion of self-righteousness, leveling the playing field and demanding humility.
4. Trusting in oneself contradicts biblical wisdom, as human hearts are inherently deceptive and prone to self-justification.
5. Jesus disrupts the narrative of righteous anger by revealing the universal guilt and calling for forgiveness and empathy instead.

Self-Reflection Questions:

1. Have I truly acknowledged my own faults and sought forgiveness, or am I still clinging to a facade of self-righteousness?

2. How does my perception of my own innocence affect my ability to empathize with others and extend forgiveness?

3. Do I trust in my own judgment and understanding, or am I willing to acknowledge the limitations of my own perspective and rely on God's wisdom?

4. Am I holding onto anger towards others based on a perceived sense of superiority or moral high ground?

5. Have I honestly confronted the truth about my own guilt and acknowledged the need for forgiveness and grace?

Life-Changing Exercises:

1. Take time each day to reflect on one area of your life where you may be holding onto anger or self-righteousness. Write down specific actions you can take to extend forgiveness and empathy towards others.
2. Engage in regular prayer or meditation to surrender the need for control and self-justification, instead inviting God's wisdom and guidance into your life.
3. Practice empathy by intentionally seeking to understand the perspectives and experiences of others, especially those with whom you may disagree or harbor resentment towards.
4. Keep a gratitude journal to cultivate a mindset of humility and thankfulness, recognizing the grace and forgiveness extended to you despite your own shortcomings.
5. Seek out opportunities to serve and support others, recognizing that true humility and righteousness are demonstrated through acts of compassion and love towards those in need.

IDEA: LET'S PUNCH BRANT IN THE FACE

In the scenario presented, there's a common urge to confront others about behaviors deemed wrong, often using means like wearing provocative T-shirts. This desire to assert moral superiority is coupled with a list of personal achievements, showcasing a perceived righteousness. However, the fundamental question isn't about these external displays of morality but rather about whether God truly loves despite one's faults. This theme is illustrated through a personal anecdote of moral failure and subsequent forgiveness, highlighting the universal truth that everyone, regardless of appearances, is flawed. The narrative emphasizes humility, acknowledging personal shortcomings, and refraining from judgment towards others. Instead of seeking to control or judge, genuine relationships are fostered through empathy and love, leaving the task of transformation to God. Ultimately, the narrative challenges the notion of self-righteousness and champions a posture of humility and grace towards others.

Key Lessons

- Attempting to assert moral superiority often leads to ineffective means of communication, such as wearing provocative T-shirts.
- External displays of moral righteousness, like listing personal achievements, may not necessarily lead to positive outcomes or admiration from others.
- People are more drawn to genuine love and empathy than displays of moral fastidiousness or superiority.
- Genuine relationships are fostered through humility, empathy, and grace towards others, rather than judgment or attempts at control.
- Refraining from being offended by others opens the door to authentic relationships and allows room for personal growth and transformation.

Self-Reflection Questions:

1. How do you tend to communicate your disapproval of others' behaviors or beliefs?

2. Have you ever found yourself trying to impress others with your moral accomplishments?

3. Do you prioritize genuine empathy and love in your interactions with others, or do you tend to judge or assert superiority?

4. How do you handle situations where you feel offended or morally superior to others?

5. In what ways can you cultivate humility and grace in your relationships with others, especially during moments of disagreement or conflict?

Life-Changing Exercises:

1. Take time to reflect on past interactions where you may have asserted moral superiority or judgment towards others. How could you have approached those situations with more empathy and grace?
2. Practice reframing your mindset from one of judgment to one of empathy and understanding when encountering behaviors or beliefs that differ from your own.
3. Engage in acts of kindness and service towards others without expecting recognition or validation for your actions.
4. Challenge yourself to actively listen to others' perspectives, even if they contradict your own beliefs or values, and seek to understand their point of view without judgment.
5. Regularly engage in self-reflection and introspection to identify areas where you can cultivate humility and grace in your interactions with others.

ATHEISTS, SOCIALISTS, AND TOAST

Initially, I believed being Christlike meant distancing oneself from others' sins. Yet, embracing others despite their sins embodies Christlikeness.

Recently, an article on Christian hip-hop artist Lecrae shed light on Christians' struggle with art, emphasizing evangelical isolationism in the 20th century. This mindset presumed non-Christians as carriers of sin, leading to separatist communities.

Personally, I once deemed it my duty to be offended by others' sins, distancing myself from their messy lives. This defensive stance contradicts Christ's example of embracing humanity amidst imperfection.

Contrary to my misconceptions, the kingdom of God isn't defensive; it's proactive, moving beyond barriers to love boldly.

Author Mike Yaconelli's anecdote about soldiers moving a cemetery fence illustrates the essence of redemption. Similarly, I aspire to move fences, welcoming everyone, regardless of differences, into a space of love and acceptance.

No longer do I aim to change people but to introduce them to a loving God. This shift in perspective fosters genuine relationships and dismantles judgmental attitudes.

Welcoming others isn't about glossing over differences but serving them with patience and love. While I've witnessed transformation, my role is to faithfully love, leaving the transformative work to God.

Understanding the Bible's redemptive arc has transformed my approach from condemnation to redemption. Instead of condemning culture, I seek its redemption.

Key Lessons

1. Scripture portrays anger as destructive, fierce, and consuming, highlighting its detrimental effects on individuals and relationships.
2. The concept of righteous anger contradicts biblical directives to rid oneself of anger, leading to hypocrisy and self-destructive behavior.
3. Surrendering self-righteousness is essential for personal growth and deeper connections with others, fostering humility and inner peace.
4. Assessing others' spiritual state is futile and judgmental, emphasizing the universal need for Jesus and humility in acknowledging our limitations.
5. Forgiveness and letting go of anger lead to inner peace and present-moment awareness, enhancing relationships and overall well-being.

Self-Reflection Questions:

1. Have you ever clung to self-righteousness, unwilling to surrender the idea that you know others' motivations and spiritual state?

2. How does the concept of righteous anger align with biblical teachings on forgiveness and humility?

3. Do you find yourself constantly assessing others' spiritual state, and how does this affect your relationships and inner peace?

4. What would it look like to surrender the need to judge others and instead embrace humility and forgiveness in your interactions?

5. How can you cultivate a deeper understanding of your own moral status before God and prioritize forgiveness and compassion in your daily life?

Life-Changing Exercises:

1. Practice letting go of the need to assess others' spiritual state or motivations for a week, focusing instead on cultivating humility and compassion in your interactions.
2. Keep a gratitude journal where you write down three things you're thankful for each day, focusing on moments of forgiveness, humility, and inner peace.
3. Engage in daily mindfulness or meditation exercises to cultivate present-moment awareness and reduce the tendency to dwell on past grievances or future judgments.
4. Reach out to someone you've been holding anger towards and offer forgiveness, even if it's just internally acknowledging your willingness to let go of resentment.
5. Reflect on passages from scripture or spiritual teachings that emphasize humility, forgiveness, and inner peace, integrating these principles into your daily life through prayer or contemplation.

ANGER'S FUN—EXCEPT FOR THE BOILING, BLAZING, AND BURNING PART

Scripture portrays anger as fierce, burning, and cruel, highlighting its destructive nature (Genesis 49:7; Exodus 11:8). Leviticus 26 equates it with hostility, while Deuteronomy 7 associates it with destruction. Yet, some advocate for righteous anger, claiming it's a gift for addressing injustice. However, this contradicts biblical directives to rid oneself of anger (Ephesians 4:31; Colossians 3:8). Surrendering self-righteousness is likened to offering a valuable gift, yet many cling to it, blind to its detrimental effects. Just as a child adores garbage, people cling to self-righteousness, reluctant to surrender it. Embracing humility and admitting uncertainty about others' spiritual state is urged, recognizing the universal need for Jesus. Assessing others' spirituality is futile; instead, focus on personal growth and reliance on God. Forgiveness and letting go of anger lead to inner peace, fostering deeper connections and presence in the moment. Surrendering the desire for righteous anger is a humble act with profound implications, offering peace and freedom from constant evaluation. God offers a better way of life, free from the burden of self-righteousness, promising peace to those who surrender their burdens to Him.

Key Lessons

1. Scripture portrays anger as destructive, fierce, and consuming, highlighting its detrimental effects on individuals and relationships.
2. The concept of righteous anger contradicts biblical directives to rid oneself of anger, leading to hypocrisy and self-destructive behavior.
3. Surrendering self-righteousness is essential for personal growth and deeper connections with others, fostering humility and inner peace.
4. Assessing others' spiritual state is futile and judgmental, emphasizing the universal need for Jesus and humility in acknowledging our limitations.

5. Forgiveness and letting go of anger lead to inner peace and present-moment awareness, enhancing relationships and overall well-being.

Self-Reflection Questions:

1. Have you ever clung to self-righteousness, unwilling to surrender the idea that you know others' motivations and spiritual state?

2. How does the concept of righteous anger align with biblical teachings on forgiveness and humility?

3. Do you find yourself constantly assessing others' spiritual state, and how does this affect your relationships and inner peace?

4. What would it look like to surrender the need to judge others and instead embrace humility and forgiveness in your interactions?

5. How can you cultivate a deeper understanding of your own moral status before God and prioritize forgiveness and compassion in your daily life?

Life-Changing Exercises:

1. Practice letting go of the need to assess others' spiritual state or motivations for a week, focusing instead on cultivating humility and compassion in your interactions.
2. Keep a gratitude journal where you write down three things you're thankful for each day, focusing on moments of forgiveness, humility, and inner peace.
3. Engage in daily mindfulness or meditation exercises to cultivate present-moment awareness and reduce the tendency to dwell on past grievances or future judgments.
4. Reach out to someone you've been holding anger towards and offer forgiveness, even if it's just internally acknowledging your willingness to let go of resentment.

5. Reflect on passages from scripture or spiritual teachings that emphasize humility, forgiveness, and inner peace, integrating these principles into your daily life through prayer or contemplation.

THE BIG QUESTION: WHAT ABOUT INJUSTICE?

The central query is: How should we respond to injustice? While anger may seem a natural reaction, it's not synonymous with action. Anger often masquerades as righteousness but can hinder true progress. Online activism, often fueled by anger, ironically leads to less real-world impact. The notion of "righteous anger" is challenged; biblical teachings emphasize love over anger in addressing injustice. Historical figures like Martin Luther King Jr. and Dietrich Bonhoeffer advocated for love-driven action, not anger. Waiting on the Lord and trusting His justice, rather than harboring self-righteous anger, is urged. While anger may momentarily feel empowering, it ultimately stems from a lack of trust in God's sovereignty. Choosing to relinquish anger doesn't mean tolerating injustice but actively pursuing justice with humility and trust in a just God.

Key Lessons

1. The common belief that anger is necessary to combat injustice is challenged, emphasizing the distinction between anger and action.
2. Confusing anger with action undermines efforts to address injustice effectively, as anger often leads to inaction or superficial engagement.
3. Motivated by love, individuals can fight injustice without relying on anger, which risks being self-righteous and counterproductive.
4. Despite occasional short-term benefits, anger is not endorsed as a solution for addressing injustice in the long term, as it often leads to negative consequences.
5. The biblical narrative and examples from figures like Martin Luther King Jr. and Dietrich Bonhoeffer highlight the importance of acting out of love rather than anger to effect positive change.

Self-Reflection Questions:

1. Have you ever conflated anger with action, believing that anger is necessary to address injustice?

2. How does your understanding of anger influence your approach to advocating for justice and engaging with social issues?

3. Reflect on instances where you've witnessed or experienced anger hindering efforts to address injustice effectively.

4. Consider how your motives for fighting injustice align with biblical principles of love and humility.

5. Are there areas in your life where you could redirect anger into constructive action motivated by love?

Life-Changing Exercises:

1. Practice discerning between anger and action by intentionally seeking opportunities to address injustice with a spirit of love and humility.
2. Engage in self-reflection to identify any underlying anger or resentment that may be hindering your ability to advocate for justice effectively.
3. Explore alternative ways to channel your passion for justice, such as volunteering, fundraising, or supporting organizations working to address social issues.
4. Cultivate a habit of waiting on the Lord when faced with injustice, trusting in His timing and ultimate justice.
5. Prioritize humility and trust in God's providence by relinquishing the need to control outcomes and embracing a posture of surrender in your pursuit of justice.

THIS IS THE CHAPTER ABOUT HOW WE'RE JUST BARELY SMART ENOUGH TO BE STUPID

In this chapter, the focus is on human peculiarity in feeling threatened without immediate danger, unlike other creatures. While animals respond to imminent threats, humans induce stress even in the absence of physical peril, which can have detrimental effects. For instance, a near miss in traffic triggers a fight-or-flight response, flooding the body with hormones like adrenaline and cortisol. This physiological reaction, intended for survival, temporarily shuts down non-essential functions like digestion and reproduction.

Humans, unlike animals, can imagine and dwell on potential threats, leading to chronic stress. This prolonged stress wreaks havoc on the body, affecting muscles, immune system, fertility, respiratory system, metabolism, and even accelerating aging at a genetic level. Despite this, humans persist in worrying and feeling threatened, often rooted in insecurity and a lack of trust in God.

The narrative contrasts human insecurity with the superficial confidence of a remarkable individual, highlighting the futility of seeking security in worldly achievements or appearances. It emphasizes the importance of trusting in God rather than seeking validation from external sources, as true security lies in being loved by God, not in worldly accomplishments. Ultimately, the chapter underscores the danger of constant threat perception and the need to trust in God for genuine peace and security.

Key Lessons

1. Humans have a unique ability to feel threatened even in the absence of immediate danger, leading to chronic stress and its detrimental effects on health.

2. Unlike animals, humans can imagine and internalize potential threats, keeping them in a perpetual state of fight-or-flight response.

3. Stress, particularly when chronic, wreaks havoc on the body, affecting muscles, immune system, digestive system, cardiovascular health, metabolism, and overall well-being.

4. Despite advancements in intelligence and technology, humans often struggle with insecurity and the quest for external validation, leading to a never-ending cycle of striving and dissatisfaction.

5. True security and contentment come from trusting in something greater than oneself, rather than seeking validation from external achievements or appearances.

Self-Reflection Questions:

1. How often do you find yourself feeling threatened or stressed about situations that are not immediate dangers?

____

____

____

____

____

____

____

____

2. What are some ways in which you internalize potential threats or create scenarios of worry in your mind?

3. In what areas of your life do you struggle with insecurity and the need for external validation?

4. How does your level of trust in something greater than yourself influence your overall sense of security and well-being?

5. Reflect on instances where you have sought validation from external achievements or appearances. How did it affect your long-term happiness and contentment?

Life-Changing Exercises:

1. Practice mindfulness meditation for at least 10 minutes each day to cultivate awareness of your thoughts and emotions, allowing you to identify and address sources of stress and insecurity.

2. Keep a gratitude journal and write down three things you are thankful for every day, focusing on aspects of your life that bring genuine joy and fulfillment beyond external achievements.

3. Engage in regular physical activity, such as walking, yoga, or swimming, to reduce stress hormones and promote relaxation and well-being.

4. Connect with a supportive community or mentor who shares your values and can provide guidance and

encouragement on your journey toward greater self-acceptance and trust.

5. Practice letting go of the need for external validation by setting meaningful personal goals that align with your values and contribute to your sense of purpose and fulfillment, independent of others' opinions or expectations.

NOTHING LEFT TO LOSE

To achieve a state of being unoffendable, one must relinquish attachment to anything that could be lost. Embracing this mindset aligns with Jesus' teachings, offering a path to a better life. Fear of losing status, appearance, wealth, or family breeds insecurity and anger. Surrendering everything, even cherished possessions or loved ones, proves challenging but necessary for genuine trust in God. The reality of suffering challenges our faith in God's protection, yet trusting Him despite uncertainty is essential. Idolizing family safety distorts priorities; true trust means valuing God above all else, even in the face of tragedy. Learning from Job's example, trusting God requires accepting mystery and believing in His goodness despite present suffering. A father's response to unimaginable loss illustrates the depth of trust in God's plan, even amid chaos. Surrendering our lives to Christ means entrusting everything, including our children, to Him. Embracing this radical trust acknowledges that God's love surpasses our own, providing solace in life's uncertainties.

Key Lessons

1. Being unoffendable requires relinquishing attachment to avoid feeling threatened.
2. Trusting God involves surrendering everything, even cherished possessions and loved ones.
3. Idolizing family safety distorts priorities and challenges genuine trust in God.
4. True trust in God means valuing Him for Himself, not just for what He provides.
5. Trusting God involves embracing mystery and believing in His goodness despite present suffering.

Self-Reflection Questions:

1. Have you ever found yourself prioritizing the safety of your family over your trust in God's plan?

2. How do you react when faced with the uncertainty of whether God will protect your loved ones?

3. Do you believe in God's goodness even when faced with tragic circumstances?

4. Have you ever idolized your family's safety or security over your relationship with God?

5. What steps can you take to deepen your trust in God, especially in times of uncertainty and suffering?

Life-Changing Exercises:

1. Reflect on a time when you felt challenged to trust God with something dear to you. Write about how you navigated that experience and what you learned from it.
2. Spend time in prayer, specifically focusing on surrendering your fears and anxieties about your family's safety to God.
3. Engage in a study of biblical figures who demonstrated trust in God despite difficult

circumstances, such as Job or Abraham. Reflect on how their stories inspire your own trust journey.

4. Practice gratitude by regularly acknowledging and thanking God for the blessings of your family, while also acknowledging that they ultimately belong to Him.

5. Consider volunteering or supporting organizations that provide aid to families in crisis, allowing you to channel your trust in God into tangible acts of love and support for others.

AND HERE'S THE CHAPTER I KEPT PUTTING OFF . . .

This chapter, long delayed, explores God's love. Despite not feeling particularly spiritual and feeling sinful, the author acknowledges that most people aren't in constant awe of God's love. However, God's love remains amazing, persistent, and unchanging, regardless of our emotional fluctuations. The author compares our distractibility to Dug the dog from "Up," easily losing focus. Despite our shortcomings, God's grace and love persist. The author recounts a humorous yet painful incident of running into a glass wall, illustrating how reality doesn't conform to our perceptions. This realization, that God's love is unchanging and not based on our performance, is liberating and contrasts sharply with societal norms. Many Christians, burdened by the belief that God is displeased with them, become easily offended. They believe in God's love but suspect it's conditional on their behavior. Like the father in Mark 9, they say, "I believe; help my unbelief!" Jesus, however, responds with compassion, not condemnation, showing that His love surpasses human understanding.

Key Lessons

1. God's love is persistent and unchanging, even when we don't feel particularly spiritual or deserving of it.
2. Despite our distractions and shortcomings, God's grace remains amazing and ever-present.
3. Our perception of reality doesn't alter the truth of God's love and presence.
4. Belief in God's unconditional love is liberating and relieves the pressure of trying to earn His favor through performance.
5. Jesus' compassionate response to our struggles and doubts demonstrates the depth of God's love and acceptance.

Self-Reflection Questions:

1. Do you often find yourself striving to earn God's love and approval through your actions?

2. How does your belief in God's unconditional love impact your daily life and relationships?

3. Are there areas in your life where you struggle to fully trust in God's love and acceptance?

4. How does the concept of God's unchanging love challenge your preconceived notions about worthiness and performance?

5. What steps can you take to cultivate a deeper awareness and appreciation of God's unwavering love in your life?

Life-Changing Exercises:

1. Spend time each day meditating on Scriptures that emphasize God's love and grace, allowing them to sink deeply into your heart and mind.
2. Keep a journal where you record moments when you tangibly experience God's love or grace in your life, no matter how small or insignificant they may seem.
3. Practice offering yourself grace and forgiveness when you fall short, recognizing that God's love is not dependent on your perfection.
4. Engage in regular conversations with trusted friends or mentors who can remind you of God's unconditional love and help you navigate doubts or struggles.
5. Consider participating in a study or group focused on exploring the depths of God's love and grace, allowing yourself to be surrounded by others who can encourage and support you on your journey.

WE'RE ALL WAITING FOR SOMETHING . . . THAT ALREADY HAPPENED

In Khaled Hosseini's novel "And the Mountains Echoed," the character Nabi reflects on life's trials, expressing a universal longing for something extraordinary to happen. Similarly, I've found myself compulsively checking my email, seeking hope and good news. We all seem to await a transformative event that will validate our significance and security. Yet, what if this extraordinary occurrence has already transpired?

Consider the traditional notion of a king, exemplified in Laurence Bergreen's account of Ferdinand Magellan's journey. Despite kings' perceived inaccessibility, the King of kings desires a personal relationship with us, offering eternal belonging and love. If we grasp this truth, it should evoke awe and joy, reshaping our responses to offense and criticism.

Sherri's experience with racism illustrates the transformative power of unconditional love. By forgiving and embracing those who wrong her, she embodies Jesus' command to love others radically. This love, surpassing familial loyalty, becomes evidence of God's existence and our belonging to Him.

Let's embrace this love, demonstrating our allegiance to Jesus by refusing to harbor offense and extending grace to all.

Key Lessons

- Despite our longing for extraordinary events, the realization of God's love and presence in our lives may have already occurred.
- God, as the King of kings, desires a personal relationship with us, offering eternal belonging and love.
- Belief in God's love should evoke awe and joy, transforming our responses to offense and criticism.

- Our love for one another becomes evidence of our faith in Jesus and our belonging to Him.
- Loving those whom we would otherwise despise, in the name of Jesus, demonstrates the profound impact of God's love on our lives.

Self-reflection questions:

1. Have you ever caught yourself longing for something extraordinary to happen in your life? What were you hoping for?

2. How does your understanding of God's love influence your reactions to offense and criticism?

3. Do you believe that God's love for you is sufficient to overcome feelings of unworthiness or insignificance?

4. Are there individuals in your life whom you struggle to love or forgive? How might your perception change if you viewed them through the lens of God's love?

5. Reflect on moments when you've experienced or witnessed unconditional love. How did it shape your understanding of God's love?

Life-changing exercises:

1. Take time each day to meditate on God's love for you. Reflect on specific instances where you've experienced His love in your life.
2. Practice forgiveness by intentionally extending grace to those who have wronged you, acknowledging that God has forgiven you.
3. Engage in acts of love and kindness towards others, especially those whom you find difficult to love. Let your actions be a reflection of God's love.
4. Keep a gratitude journal to document moments of God's love and provision in your life, cultivating a heart of thankfulness.
5. Seek out opportunities to share your faith and God's love with others, whether through acts of service, words

of encouragement, or simply being present for someone in need.

ON WINNING—AND BY "WINNING," I MEAN, OF COURSE, LOSING

Since college, I've been known as "Argument Guy," always engaging in debates. Whether in class or with teachers, I couldn't resist arguing. However, I've realized that without love, my arguments are futile. Jesus' emphasis on love challenges me to extend it even to those I disagree with. Forgiveness, though difficult, is essential, as it mirrors God's forgiveness of us. Letting go of anger means sacrificing our sense of justice, but it's necessary for true freedom. Jesus demands radical forgiveness, not just lip service. Despite struggles, I'm learning to be patient and empathetic, even in heated exchanges. Recognizing God's sovereignty frees me from the need to "win" arguments, allowing me to respond with grace. This shift in perspective brings peace and liberation from anger and guilt.

Key Lessons

- The author has always been known as "Argument Guy," someone who enjoys engaging in debates and discussions.
- Despite his love for logic and argument, he acknowledges that without love, his arguments are futile.
- The author reflects on the importance of forgiveness and letting go of offense, recognizing the sacrifice it entails.
- Jesus' command to forgive as we have been forgiven challenges societal norms of holding onto anger.
- The author shares personal struggles with patience and forgiveness but acknowledges growth in handling disagreements with grace.

Self-reflection questions:

1. Have you ever found yourself engaging in arguments or debates for the sake of it, without considering the impact on relationships?

---

2. How does the concept of forgiveness challenge your sense of justice and desire for retribution?

3. Reflect on a time when you struggled to forgive someone. What beliefs or attitudes prevented you from extending forgiveness?

4. In what ways do societal norms influence your response to offense and anger? How does Jesus' example challenge these norms?

5. Consider moments when you've experienced growth in patience and forgiveness. What factors contributed

to this growth, and how can you continue to cultivate these qualities?

Life-changing exercises:

1. Practice pausing before responding in disagreements or arguments, allowing space for empathy and understanding.

2. Keep a forgiveness journal to track instances where you've chosen to forgive, reflecting on the emotional and spiritual benefits.
3. Engage in acts of kindness towards those who have wronged you, recognizing that forgiveness is a continual process.
4. Seek out opportunities for reconciliation and dialogue with individuals with whom you've had conflicts, focusing on understanding and forgiveness.
5. Spend time in prayer and meditation, asking for God's help in releasing anger and embracing forgiveness in your relationships.

THE WORLD'S WORST NEIGHBOR

I'm the worst neighbor. Socially awkward, I struggle to connect with those around me. Even when tragedy struck my neighbor Andrea, I failed to notice. Her husband Jarrod lost her in a car accident, leaving him and their son alone. Despite my discomfort, I decided to reach out to Jarrod. Surprisingly, he welcomed me in and shared his grief. Over time, I kept visiting him, offering support despite his unpredictable emotions. It wasn't easy, but I realized this act of love was essential. Being unoffendable became my ministry, inspired by Jesus' example of bearing wounds for others. It's not about seeking approval but freely loving others, even when it's challenging. This mindset transformed my interactions, allowing me to be present for Jarrod in his darkest moments.

Key Lessons

1. Social awkwardness and introversion can hinder meaningful connections with neighbors, requiring intentional effort to overcome.
2. Tragedy often reveals the importance of reaching out and offering support to those in need, even if it feels uncomfortable.
3. Choosing to be unoffendable is a crucial aspect of ministry, allowing individuals to bear the wounds of others without becoming alienated.
4. Genuine ministry involves serving others without seeking approval or validation from them.
5. Being unoffendable frees individuals to love others deeply and selflessly, transcending personal discomfort and insecurity.

Self-Reflection Questions:

1. Are you willing to step out of your comfort zone to offer support and love to those in need, even if it feels awkward or challenging?

---

2. How do you react when faced with situations that require reaching out to others who may be experiencing hardship or tragedy?

3. Do you find yourself seeking validation or approval from others in your acts of service and ministry?

4. How do you handle criticism or rejection when offering support and love to others?

5. In what ways can you cultivate a mindset of being unoffendable in your interactions with those around you?

Life-Changing Exercises:

1. Practice intentional acts of kindness and support towards your neighbors or those in your community, regardless of any discomfort or insecurity you may feel.

2. Keep a journal documenting your experiences and reflections as you strive to be unoffendable in your interactions with others, noting any challenges and growth opportunities.
3. Engage in regular self-reflection sessions where you examine your motives and attitudes towards serving others, seeking to align them with a genuine desire to love selflessly.
4. Seek feedback from trusted friends or mentors about your approach to ministry and service, inviting constructive criticism to help you grow in being unoffendable.
5. Dedicate time each day to meditate or pray on the example of Jesus, reflecting on how His unoffendable love can inspire and empower you to love others more deeply and authentically.

IMBALANCED? YOU BETTER HOPE SO

The story recounts a series of misfortunes stemming from the narrator's mistake of filling their diesel car with regular gas. This led to costly repairs and a back injury. Despite feeling deserving of punishment, Volkswagen surprisingly covered all expenses. However, the narrator struggles with the concept of receiving grace without "paying the price." They explore the discomfort of not being held accountable and the inherent unfairness of grace. The narrative delves into the tension between human notions of fairness and the imbalanced nature of grace, as exemplified by Jesus' parables. The author challenges the idea of earning righteousness through religious acts and emphasizes the offensive yet liberating nature of grace. They conclude that while grace may defy common sense and balance, it offers profound freedom from self-righteousness.

Key Lessons

1. The narrator recounts a series of unfortunate events stemming from their own mistakes, leading to feelings of guilt and failure.
2. Despite expecting to pay the price for their errors, they receive unexpected grace from Volkswagen, prompting mixed emotions of gratitude and discomfort.
3. The concept of grace challenges conventional notions of fairness and balance, highlighting its imbalanced nature in contrast to worldly standards.
4. The narrator reflects on the offensive nature of grace, which defies the idea of earning righteousness through religious or moral works.
5. Scripture underscores the disruptive nature of grace, causing religious individuals to stumble over the notion of being justified through faith rather than works.

Self-Reflection Questions:

1. How do you typically respond when faced with the consequences of your mistakes or errors?

2. Have you ever experienced unexpected grace or forgiveness in a situation where you felt you deserved punishment or consequences?

3. What emotions arise when you consider the concept of grace and its implications for fairness and justice?

4. Do you find it challenging to accept grace when it contradicts your sense of deserving based on your actions or efforts?

5. In what ways do you perceive grace as offensive or disruptive to conventional religious or moral beliefs?

Life-Changing Exercises:

1. Reflect on past experiences where you received grace or forgiveness despite feeling undeserving, noting the impact it had on your emotions and beliefs.
2. Engage in conversations with others about their understanding of grace and its role in their lives, exploring different perspectives and interpretations.
3. Challenge yourself to let go of the need for balance or fairness in certain situations, embracing the imbalanced nature of grace with humility and gratitude.
4. Study scripture passages related to grace and righteousness, seeking to deepen your understanding of how grace challenges and transforms traditional religious paradigms.
5. Practice extending grace to others in your interactions and relationships, even when they may seem undeserving or have not met your expectations, recognizing the liberating power of grace in fostering compassion and forgiveness.

I CAN WORSHIP A GOD LIKE THAT

In a diner in Honolulu, Tony Campolo encountered a group of prostitutes, including Agnes, on her birthday. He organized a surprise party for her the next night. Despite initial skepticism, the event was a success, touching Agnes deeply. Later, Tony joined a relief effort in Indonesia after a tsunami. Despite threats and initial resistance, they provided aid and comfort, earning the trust of locals, even an imam who invited them to dinner. Tony reflects on the transformative power of love and grace, citing Jesus's example of embracing the marginalized and broken. He contrasts this with attempts to create artificial environments devoid of challenges, emphasizing the importance of engaging with the world as it is. He concludes by discussing personal growth and the pursuit of genuine connections over superficial achievements. Ultimately, he finds inspiration in a God who humbly embraces humanity's brokenness, exemplified by Jesus's willingness to dwell among the marginalized and rejected.

Key Lessons

1. Grace has the power to change hearts in ways that rules cannot.
2. Love and forgiveness, even in the face of hostility, can lead to profound transformations.
3. Embracing discomfort and vulnerability can open doors to unexpected connections and opportunities for love.
4. Avoiding conflict and living in a bubble of safety is contrary to the world Jesus came to save.
5. True freedom comes from letting go of anger and embracing a life of love and presence with others.

Self-Reflection Questions:

1. How do I respond to people who challenge or offend me, and can I find freedom in choosing love and forgiveness instead of anger?

2. In what areas of my life do I prioritize comfort and safety over vulnerability and connection with others?

3. Am I willing to embrace discomfort and uncertainty in order to pursue meaningful relationships and opportunities for love?

4. How can I let go of my desire for status and significance in order to prioritize loving and serving others?

5. Do I truly understand the depth of God's love and grace, and am I allowing it to transform my heart and relationships?

Life-Changing Exercises:

1. Practice forgiveness by intentionally letting go of any lingering anger or resentment towards someone who has hurt you.
2. Step out of your comfort zone by volunteering in a challenging or unfamiliar environment, such as a homeless shelter or disaster relief organization.
3. Engage in active listening and presence with others by spending time getting to know someone new without any agenda or distractions.
4. Reflect on areas of your life where you prioritize status or success, and consider ways to shift your focus towards serving and loving others.
5. Spend time meditating on the example of Jesus, who demonstrated radical love and humility in his interactions with others, and strive to emulate his compassion and grace in your own life.

HERE'S THE PART WHERE I TALK ABOUT SOME DANISH PEOPLE

In the captivating film "Babette's Feast," set in a foggy Danish fishing village, two sisters lead a joyless life under their strict father's religious teachings. When a refugee maid, Babette, wins the lottery, she uses her winnings to prepare an extravagant meal for the community. Despite initial discomfort, the guests, led by the sisters, reluctantly partake. As they savor the exquisite dishes, joy overwhelms them, realizing Babette's act as pure grace. This tale underscores the challenge of accepting unmerited blessings, akin to embracing God's grace despite its perceived unfairness. Likewise, embracing humility entails trusting in God's abundant grace, freeing oneself from guilt and the need for control. The story echoes the struggle of reconciling human inadequacy with divine grace, urging humility and acceptance. Ultimately, it highlights the choice between offense and embracing the unfathomable generosity of God's kingdom, encouraging a childlike acceptance of divine gifts and the joy they bring.

Key Lessons

1. "Babette's Feast" depicts the transformational power of grace through a lavish meal prepared by a refugee turned chef for a joyless religious community.
2. Embracing God's grace requires humility and acceptance of the seemingly unfair blessings He bestows.
3. Jesus' sacrifice covers all sins, freeing believers from guilt and condemnation.
4. Living in humility means trusting in God's grace and letting go of the need to measure up or control everything.
5. Accepting the scandalous grace of the kingdom leads to freedom and joy in embracing God's gifts without reservation.

Self-Reflection Questions:

1. How do I respond to God's grace in moments when it feels undeserved or unfair?

2. Am I able to let go of guilt and condemnation, trusting fully in Jesus' sacrifice for my salvation?

3. Do I struggle with the need to control or measure up in my relationship with God and others?

4. How can I cultivate a greater sense of humility and acceptance of God's grace in my life?

5. In what ways do I resist the scandalous generosity of God's kingdom, and how can I learn to embrace it more fully?

Life-Changing Exercises:

1. Practice letting go of guilt and self-condemnation by meditating on the completeness of Jesus' sacrifice and forgiveness.
2. Reflect on areas of your life where you struggle to trust God's grace and surrender control, and commit to letting go of those burdens.
3. Engage in acts of humility and service, focusing on loving others without expectation of recognition or reward.
4. Explore ways to embrace the scandalous generosity of God's kingdom by extending grace and forgiveness to those who have wronged you.
5. Spend time in prayer and reflection, asking God to reveal areas of pride or self-reliance that hinder your ability to fully accept His grace and love.

FORGET DANISH PEOPLE—LET'S TALK ABOUT YOUR ELBOW

Let's shift our focus from Danish people to something closer to home—your elbow. You probably weren't thinking about it until now, unless it's injured or causing you discomfort. That's the thing about physical discomfort—it demands attention. Similarly, Timothy Keller draws parallels between an inflamed joint and the human ego. When our egos are oversized, we're hyper-aware of ourselves, constantly bracing for injury. True humility isn't self-deprecation but self-forgetfulness.

Consider my grandma in her eighties; she exuded a carefree attitude toward others' opinions. Unlike the lady with grandiose plans to save the world, my grandma wasn't concerned with significance. While society applauds visionary leaders, the Bible highlights the humility of the least likely candidates. Ants, with no hierarchy, exemplify efficient teamwork, devoid of individual glory.

Humility isn't about denying oneself but recognizing a higher purpose beyond personal significance. Sokreaksa Himm's journey from rage to forgiveness illustrates this beautifully. True humility is remembering God's sovereignty, acknowledging our interconnectedness, and relinquishing entitlement to anger. It's not about emptying the mind but filling it with the awareness of something greater at work in the world.

Key Lessons

1. Real humility lies in self-forgetfulness, not self-denigration.
2. Constantly being hurt, offended, or angered may indicate an inflated ego.
3. Humility means being unoffendable and sacrificing oneself for others.
4. God often chooses the humble and unlikely to accomplish remarkable things.

5. Forgiveness and letting go of anger are essential components of humility and emotional health.

Self-Reflection Questions:

1. How often do you find yourself being hurt, offended, or angered by situations or people?

2. In what areas of your life do you think your ego might be inflated, and how does it affect your interactions with others?

3. What steps can you take to cultivate a more humble attitude and practice self-forgetfulness in your daily life?

4. Have you ever struggled with forgiveness or holding onto anger? How did it impact you, and what did you learn from the experience?

5. How can you shift your focus from self-centered thoughts to considering others and their perspectives more deeply?

Life-Changing Exercises:

1. Practice forgiveness: Identify someone you're holding onto resentment or anger towards, and make a conscious effort to forgive them, even if it's challenging.
2. Keep a gratitude journal: Each day, write down three things you're thankful for. This practice can help shift your focus away from yourself and towards gratitude for what you have.
3. Serve others anonymously: Find a way to help someone without seeking recognition or praise for your actions. This exercise can help cultivate humility and a genuine desire to serve.
4. Practice active listening: In conversations, focus on truly listening to the other person without interrupting or thinking about your response. This exercise can help you become more attentive to others' needs and perspectives.

5. Reflect on your strengths and weaknesses: Take time to honestly assess your strengths and weaknesses, acknowledging areas where you may need to grow or change. This reflection can help foster humility and a realistic self-awareness.

AND LO, THE KINGDOM OF GOD IS LIKE A TERRIBLE FOOTBALL TEAM

My child, much like me, isn't keen on sports. Nevertheless, we enrolled him in a flag football league in sixth grade. My wife informed me they needed a coach for his team, the Rams, but I adamantly refused; coaching football wasn't my forte. Despite my clear stance, the park district persisted in asking, to which I repeatedly declined. Upon dropping my son off at practice, the kids mistook me for their coach, to which I initially denied, opting to play catch instead. However, a persistent boy named Jared asked if he could call me "Coach" for the day. Reluctantly, I agreed, unknowingly committing to coach the Rams.

Throughout the season, we faced defeat after defeat, unable to score a single point. Our practices were modest compared to the well-equipped Yellow Shirt Team, leaving us feeling inadequate. Despite our struggles, we faced the Yellow Team in our final game, with a surprising turn of events as we scored the opening touchdown. Although short-lived, this victory highlighted the unpredictable nature of football.

The conclusion of our season brought an unexpected twist as a limousine arrived for the Rams' end-of-season celebration, transforming our dejected team into triumphant champions. This unforeseen turn of events mirrors the workings of the kingdom of God, where the least expected often emerge as victors. It's a reminder that our efforts and performance pale in comparison to the divine plan, where humility and trust in God's guidance lead to ultimate success.

Key Lessons

1. Reluctantly coaching a flag-football team, the author's lack of expertise led to initial refusal but eventual acceptance.
2. Despite their team's poor performance, an unexpected victory brought joy and transformed the players' perception.

3. The author draws parallels between the football experience and the workings of the kingdom of God, emphasizing humility and the unexpected nature of success.
4. Choosing to be unoffendable leads to humility, joy, and a deeper understanding of faith.
5. An anecdote about a confusing car trip highlights the importance of trust and humility in accepting God's guidance.

Self-Reflection Questions:

1. Have you ever found yourself in a situation where you felt unqualified or reluctant to take on a responsibility? How did you handle it?

2. Reflect on a time when you experienced unexpected success or joy despite initial challenges or setbacks. What lessons did you learn from that experience?

3. How does the author's comparison between the football team's journey and the kingdom of God resonate with your understanding of faith and humility?

4. In what ways do you struggle with being unoffendable or relinquishing control in your life? How can you cultivate a deeper sense of trust in God's guidance?

____

____

____

____

____

____

____

____

5. Consider the anecdote about the car trip. How does it relate to your own journey of faith and trust in God's plan?

____

Life-Changing Exercises:

1. Take on a new challenge or responsibility that pushes you out of your comfort zone. Embrace the opportunity to learn and grow despite initial reluctance or self-doubt.

2. Practice letting go of the need to control outcomes or situations in your life. Trust in God's guidance and timing, even when things seem uncertain.
3. Cultivate a spirit of humility by actively seeking opportunities to serve others without seeking recognition or praise.
4. Reflect on past experiences of unexpected joy or success, and consider how they have shaped your perspective on faith and trust in God.
5. Spend time in prayer and meditation, focusing on surrendering your own desires and plans to God's will. Allow yourself to rest in the knowledge that God's love and guidance are constant, even in uncertain times.

SELF EVALUATION

Congratulations on completing the workbook! You've taken an important step in your personal growth journey, and I commend you for your commitment to self-improvement. As you reflect on your journey through this workbook, it's essential to assess your progress and identify areas for further development. Here are 12 self-evaluation questions to help you evaluate your experience:

1. Did I engage actively with the content of the workbook, or did I simply go through the motions?

2. How effectively did I apply the principles and strategies outlined in the workbook to my own life?

3. Did I take the time to reflect deeply on the questions and prompts provided, or did I rush through them?

4. To what extent did I implement the recommended exercises and practices into my daily routine?

5. Did I encounter any challenges or obstacles while working through the workbook, and how did I overcome them?

6. Did I seek feedback or support from others as I progressed through the workbook, or did I attempt to navigate it alone?

7. How consistent was my commitment to self-reflection and introspection throughout the workbook?

8. Did I notice any changes in my attitudes, behaviors, or perspectives as a result of completing the workbook? If so, what were they?

9. What were the most valuable insights or lessons I gained from working through the workbook?

10. In what areas do I still feel I have room for improvement or further growth?

11. How can I incorporate the principles and practices learned from the workbook into my long-term personal development plan?

12. Looking back, what would I do differently if I were to go through the workbook again, and how can I apply these insights moving forward?

By honestly reflecting on these questions, you can gain valuable insights into your progress, identify areas for growth, and set yourself up for continued success on your journey toward self-improvement. Remember, self-awareness and ongoing reflection are key ingredients in personal transformation. Best of luck on your continued path of growth and development!

Made in the USA
Middletown, DE
09 September 2024

60613957R00116